GEO

ENDANGERED AND THREATENED ANIMALS

THE WOODLAND CARIBOU

A MyReportLinks.com Book

Amy Graham and William Haslam

MyReportLinks.com Books

an imprint of

Enslow Publishers, Inc.

Box 398, 40 Industrial Road
Berkeley Heights, NJ 07922
USA

MyReportLinks.com Books, an imprint of Enslow Publishers, Inc. MyReportLinks is a trademark of Enslow Publishers, Inc.

Library of Congress Cataloging-in-Publication Data

Graham, Amy.
    The woodland caribou / Amy Graham and William Haslam.
        p. cm. — (Endangered and threatened animals)
    Summary: Discusses what woodland caribou are, why they are endangered, what their current status is, and what is being done to help them. Includes Internet links to Web sites related to woodland caribou.
    Includes bibliographical references (p.   ) and index.
    ISBN 0-7660-5054-8
    1. Woodland caribou—Juvenile literature. 2. Endangered species—Juvenile literature. [1. Woodland caribou. 2. Caribou. 3. Endangered species.] I. Haslam, William. II. Title. III. Series.
QL737.U55 G725 2003
599.65'8—dc21

                                        2002008753

Printed in the United States of America

10 9 8 7 6 5 4 3 2 1

To Our Readers:
Through the purchase of this book, you and your library gain access to the Report Links that specifically back up this book.
The Publisher will provide access to the Report Links that back up this book and will keep these Report Links up to date on **www.myreportlinks.com** for three years from the book's first publication date.
We have done our best to make sure all Internet addresses in this book were active and appropriate when we went to press. However, the author and the Publisher have no control over, and assume no liability for, the material available on those Internet sites or on other Web sites they may link to.
The usage of the MyReportLinks.com Books Web site is subject to the terms and conditions stated on the Usage Policy Statement on **www.myreportlinks.com**.
In the future, a password may be required to access the Report Links that back up this book. The password is found on the bottom of page 4 of this book.
Any comments or suggestions can be sent by e-mail to comments@myreportlinks.com or to the address on the back cover.

Photo Credits: Alberta Fish and Wildlife, p. 11; Click Art, p. 10; © Bert Gildart, pp. 20, 32, 34, 35; © Corel Corporation, pp. 1, 3, 13, 26, 38, 41; eNature.com, p. 25; infonorth.org, p. 17; John Bavaro, p. 22; MyReportLinks.com Books, p. 4; NWT Wildlife and Fisheries, p. 29; Saskatchewan Interactive, pp. 15, 28; U.S. Fish and Wildlife Service, p. 44; Washington Department of Fish and Wildlife, pp. 19, 37, 40, 42.

Cover Photo: © Bert Gildart

Contents

MyReportLinks.com Books
Great Books, Great Links, Great for Research!

MyReportLinks.com Books present the information you need to learn about your report subject. In addition, they show you where to go on the Internet for more information. The pre-evaluated Report Links that back up this book are kept up to date on **www.myreportlinks.com**. With the purchase of a MyReportLinks.com Books title, you and your library gain access to the Report Links that specifically back up that book. The Report Links save hours of research time and link to dozens—even hundreds—of Web sites, source documents, and photos related to your report topic.

Please see "To Our Readers" on the Copyright page for important information about this book, the MyReportLinks.com Books Web site, and the Report Links that back up this book.

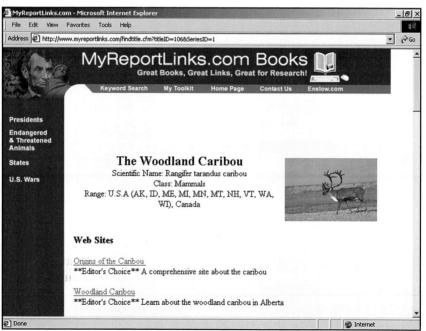

Access:

The Publisher will provide access to the Report Links that back up this book and will try to keep these Report Links up to date on our Web site for three years from the book's first publication date. Please enter **EWC1571** if asked for a password.

Report Links

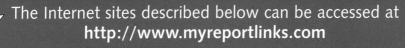

The Internet sites described below can be accessed at
http://www.myreportlinks.com

*EDITOR'S CHOICE

Origins of the Caribou

The Caribou Quebec Foundation explores in detail the origins, ecology, and other interesting aspects of the caribou. You will also learn about the caribou's physical characteristics and the role they play in the caribou's habitat.

Link to this Internet site from http://www.myreportlinks.com

*EDITOR'S CHOICE

Woodland Caribou

At this Web site you will learn about the distribution of the woodland caribou in Alberta and factors affecting the caribou's habitat. You will also find out about the woodland caribou's status and the progress being made through conservation management.

Link to this Internet site from http://www.myreportlinks.com

*EDITOR'S CHOICE

Bagheera

The Bagheera Web site dedicated to educating individuals about endangered species, the extinction crisis, pollution, habitat loss, over exploitation, and other issues.

Link to this Internet site from http://www.myreportlinks.com

*EDITOR'S CHOICE

Endangered! Exploring a World at Risk

By navigating through this Web site you can explore a variety of issues relating to endangered species and habitats. In particular, you will learn about the woodland caribou, the pronghorn, and the American bison.

Link to this Internet site from http://www.myreportlinks.com

*EDITOR'S CHOICE

Woodland Caribou

At this Web site you will learn about the physical attributes and status of the Woodland caribou. Information about the Woodland caribou's habitat, behavior, diet, and conservation efforts is also included.

Link to this Internet site from http://www.myreportlinks.com

*EDITOR'S CHOICE

Caribou

At this Web site you will learn about the distribution of the woodland caribou in North America. You will also learn about the different species of the caribou, its migration habits, threats, and conservation efforts.

Link to this Internet site from http://www.myreportlinks.com

		STOP					
Back	Forward	Stop	Review	Home	Explore	Favorites	Histor

Report Links

 The Internet sites described below can be accessed at
http://www.myreportlinks.com

▶ Animals of the NWT

At this Web site you will find detailed information about the caribou and bison. Topics discussed include history, distribution, behavior, habitat, reproduction, mortality, status, and future.

Link to this Internet site from http://www.myreportlinks.com

▶ Beetles, Parks, and Woodland Caribou

At this Web site you will find an article exploring the possible effects of the West's widespread mountain pine beetle epidemic on the Woodland caribou. Here you will learn that the greatest impact probably comes not from the epidemic itself but from human involvement.

Link to this Internet site from http://www.myreportlinks.com

▶ Biological Data and Habitat Requirements

By navigating through this list you will find information about the caribou, bison, pronghorn, and bighorn sheep. Each overview contains an introduction, information about the distribution and occurrence of the mammal, biological data, habitat requirements, and other details.

Link to this Internet site from http://www.myreportlinks.com

▶ Bush Administration and Conservation

From the National Wildlife Federation, comes an article discussing the Bush Administration's energy policy and how it affects national public lands. Highlighted in this article are public land that should remain off limits to developers and the endangered animals that inhabit these lands.

Link to this Internet site from http://www.myreportlinks.com

▶ Caribou in British Columbia

This Web site explores the taxonomy and distribution, appearance, life history, food habits, behavior, and management of the woodland caribou in British Columbia.

Link to this Internet site from http://www.myreportlinks.com

▶ Caribou: *Rangifer tarandus caribou*

This Web site offers a brief history of the Caribou's introduction to the United States, their characteristics, and how they have adapted to their environment.

Link to this Internet site from http://www.myreportlinks.com

Report Links

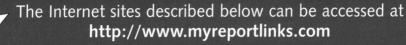

The Internet sites described below can be accessed at
http://www.myreportlinks.com

Caribou & Reindeer
This Web site provides a brief overview of some of the differences
between the caribou and reindeer.

Link to this Internet site from http://www.myreportlinks.com

Endangered Species
The Audubon Web site provides information about the Endangered
Species Act. Here you will learn what makes a species endangered or
threatened, and how a species becomes a candidate.

Link to this Internet site from http://www.myreportlinks.com

The Endangered Species Program
The Endangered Species Program provides extensive information
about endangered species. Learn about national and international
laws and policies regarding endangered species, the management of
endangered species, and more.

Link to this Internet site from http://www.myreportlinks.com

Habitat Utilization by Woodland Caribou in Northeastern Ontario
This Web site describes efforts to better understand caribou habitat
utilization and the impact of human related land use on the caribou in
the northeast region of Ontario.

Link to this Internet site from http://www.myreportlinks.com

►Hoofed Mammals
By navigating through this Web site you will learn basic facts about
hoofed mammals. Some featured endangered species are the woodland
caribou, the white-tailed deer, the pronghorn, the key deer, and others.

Link to this Internet site from http://www.myreportlinks.com

Mountain Caribou Recovery
The only remaining woodland caribou are found in the Selkirk
Mountains of Idaho, Washington, and British Columbia. The Washington
Department of Fish and Wildlife site provides a brief overview of the
program supporting recovery of the caribou in these areas.

Link to this Internet site from http://www.myreportlinks.com

 The Internet sites described below can be accessed at
http://www.myreportlinks.com

▶**NWT Wood Bison**

Today the wood bison, the northern cousin of the plains bison, is found in western Canada and parts of Alaska. At this Web site you will find a detailed profile of the wood bison and the threats it faces in its present range.

Link to this Internet site from http://www.myreportlinks.com

▶**Porcupine Caribou Herd**

At this Web site you will learn about Porcupine caribou migration and calving, and how the coastal plain is very important to caribou calving success.

Link to this Internet site from http://www.myreportlinks.com

▶**Protecting Woodland Caribou**

At this Web site you will learn about efforts to protect the woodland caribou in the Selkirk Mountains of north Idaho and some of the threats facing the woodland caribou in the winter.

Link to this Internet site from http://www.myreportlinks.com

▶**Rangifer tarandus**

The Animal Diversity Web site provides facts about the Woodland Caribou. Here you will learn about its geographic range, physical characteristics, natural history, behavior, habitat, and other interesting facts about the Woodland caribou.

Link to this Internet site from http://www.myreportlinks.com

▶*Rangifer tarandus caribou*

At this Web site you will find a brief description of the Woodland Caribou. You will also learn about environmental policy in Washington State.

Link to this Internet site from http://www.myreportlinks.com

▶**Secretive and Rare: The Woodland Caribou**

This Web site relates the story of a researcher's study on the ecology of the Woodland caribou in Saskatchewan. Here you will learn about the life and behavior of the caribou. You will also learn about the variety of threats the caribou faces.

Link to this Internet site from http://www.myreportlinks.com

Any comments? Contact us: **comments@myreportlinks.com**

Report Links

 The Internet sites described below can be accessed at
http://www.myreportlinks.com

Woodland Caribou
The Wildland's League provides a brief overview of the Woodland Caribou's habitat and threats.

Link to this Internet site from http://www.myreportlinks.com

Woodland Caribou
Alberta's Threatened Wildlife Web site provides information about the Woodland Caribou. Here you will learn about the caribous' status, habitat, behavior, management, and limiting factors.

Link to this Internet site from http://www.myreportlinks.com

▶Woodland Caribou
This site provides a brief overview of the woodland caribou. Here you will learn about its endangered status, habitat, historic range, threats, population. There is also a brief description of the woodland caribou's characteristics.

Link to this Internet site from http://www.myreportlinks.com

▶Woodland Caribou
This Web site explores the habitat of the woodland caribou. The site also tells about the many threats the caribou faces, and the attempts to conserve the woodland caribou's habitat.

Link to this Internet site from http://www.myreportlinks.com

Woodland Caribou
At this Web site you will find a brief description of the woodland caribou, where you will learn about its status, population, threats, and how it survives. You will also find links to national parks where caribou are found.

Link to this Internet site from http://www.myreportlinks.com

Woodland Caribou Dawson's subspecies
This Web site provides a brief overview of the Woodland caribou, its habitat, threats, and population and distribution.

Link to this Internet site from http://www.myreportlinks.com

Status
Endangered as of
January 14, 1983

Length*
(tip of nose to tip of tail)
Males, or bulls:
5 to 6 1/2 feet
(1.5 to 2 m)
Females, or cows:
4 1/2 to 6 feet
(1.4 to 1.8 m)

Height*
(at the shoulder)
3 1/2 feet (1.06 m)

Weight*
Bulls: 300 to 600 pounds
(136.1 to 272.2 kg)
Cows: 150 to 350 pounds
(68 to 158.8 kg)

Antlers* (1.5 m)
Bulls: 5 feet maximum
Cows: 1 1/2 feet
maximum (.45 m)

Life Span
4 1/2 years; fifteen years
maximum in wild

Pelage
(coat of fur)
Usually medium-brown or
gray (can vary widely from
black to white); whitish
underbelly, neck, and
rump; no spots at birth.

Figures represent average measurements.

Breeding Season
Early to mid-October

Gestation Period*
7 months

Number of Young
1 calf in late May or June

Current North American Range
Canada and the Selkirk
Mountains of Idaho and
Washington in the United
States

Herd Size*
4 to 50 during
mating season

Territory Size*
20 to 60 miles
(32.2 to 96.6 km)

Travel Speed*
37 to 50 miles per hour
(59.5 to 80.5 m)

Food
Variety of plants and
lichens

Common Predators
Wolves, bears,
cougars, lynx

Threats to Survival
Habitat loss

The Vanishing Caribou

On a quiet, wintry mountainside, a small band of woodland caribou roams beneath the trees. The large animals walk gracefully on top of the deep snow. They have wide, round hooves that keep them from sinking. One of the bulls lifts up its neck to eat some lichen from the tree branches. Beneath its chin is an impressive,

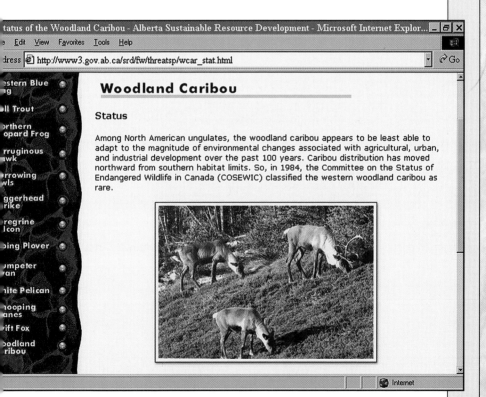

Status of the Woodland Caribou - Alberta Sustainable Resource Development - Microsoft Internet Explor...

File Edit View Favorites Tools Help

Address http://www3.gov.ab.ca/srd/fw/threatsp/wcar_stat.html Go

Western Blue ?g
ll Trout
orthern
opard Frog
rruginous
wk
rrowing
wls
ggerhead
rike
regrine
lcon
bing Plover
mpeter
an
nite Pelican
nooping
anes
ift Fox
oodland
ribou

Woodland Caribou

Status

Among North American ungulates, the woodland caribou appears to be least able to adapt to the magnitude of environmental changes associated with agricultural, urban, and industrial development over the past 100 years. Caribou distribution has moved northward from southern habitat limits. So, in 1984, the Committee on the Status of Endangered Wildlife in Canada (COSEWIC) classified the western woodland caribou as rare.

Internet

▲ Due to its inability to adapt easily to an ever-changing environment, the woodland caribou became listed as an endangered species.

shaggy growth of white fur called a *dewlap*. In the summer, the bull had a great rack of antlers but shed them for the winter. When the weather warms in the spring, the bull will grow a new pair.

Chances are good that few people have seen the woodland caribou. At one time, many of them roamed the northern forests of the United States from Maine to Washington.[1] As people settled the land, these shy animals began to disappear. Now, only one small herd of thirty caribou remains in the lower forty-eight states.

Caribou belong to a *class* of animals called mammals. Mammals are warm-blooded animals that give birth to live babies. Humans are mammals, too. Unlike humans, though, caribou have hooves and antlers. These physical features make them part of the deer *family* (scientific name *Cervidae*). Moose and elk are other members of this family of animals.

The woodland caribou does look a bit like a white-tailed deer, and a bit like a moose or an elk. Woodland caribou most closely resemble their smaller cousins, the reindeer. Reindeer live in northern Europe and Asia. Both reindeer and caribou have special wide hooves that help them walk on the snow.

Biologists have scientific names for each kind of animal. This name identifies the *species* to which the animal belongs. The scientific name of the woodland caribou is *Rangifer tarandus caribou*. All caribou and reindeer belong to the same species: *Rangifer tarandus*. The final word of the scientific name (caribou) is the *subspecies*. Animals that are very much alike, but not identical, belong to the same species but different subspecies.

A few wild woodland caribou, the last ones in the continental United States, live in the Selkirk Mountains

▲ *Wolves are among the main predators of the woodland caribou.*

of northern Idaho and northeastern Washington. More woodland caribou live farther north in Canada. Yet their numbers are also shrinking. In 1983, the U.S. Fish and Wildlife Service announced that the woodland caribou had become an endangered species in the United States. A species is considered endangered when it is threatened with extinction, or dying out.

Biologists are studying the woodland caribou and its *habitat.* A habitat is the land, water, food, and other factors that make up an animal's home. The biologists hope to find out why there are so few caribou. If we can understand what the caribou need, then we can help them to survive. People have many different ideas about why caribou are vanishing. Some feel caribou can only find food in a few old forests that have not been logged. Others

think predators like wolves and mountain lions are behind the problem of caribou survival.

Everyone agrees about one thing: the caribou's habitat is changing. People are the number one cause of habitat changes. Not many of us live in caribou habitat, but we use its forests. We harvest the trees that grow there. We extract and use the coal, oil, and natural gas found underground. We ride snowmobiles over the caribou's winter range. The caribou do not seem to be able to adjust to the changes we have made to their habitat.

Overhunting is another reason for the plight of woodland caribou. People have always hunted animals for food and sport. The early American settlers from Europe thought they had reached a land of plenty. They did not think that someday the animals might not be around. This was the fate of the huge, shaggy bison, or buffalo. In the past, all North American and European bison were commonly referred to as buffalo.

Two hundred years ago, millions of bison roamed North America. Plains bison roamed the continental United States while wood bison ranged to the north in Canada and Alaska. Professional hunters, settlers, and thrill seekers drove the bison to near extinction. Today, plains bison and wood bison number in the thousands, not millions.

Luckily, now there are laws to protect endangered species such as bison and woodland caribou. Biologists study these animals and their habitats. They try to determine why the animals are disappearing. Then the biologists write a recovery plan for each species of animal. The plan outlines what the animal needs and what we must do to help the animal survive.

What Is the Woodland Caribou?

The woodland caribou is just one of four subspecies of caribou that live in North America—woodland, barren ground, Peary's, and tundra. The best known of the North American caribou is the barren ground caribou of the far north. Barren ground caribou live in huge herds on the wide-open, arctic tundra. They travel as far as seven

▲ The caribou's coat of hollow hair provides insulation and protection from the winter elements.

hundred miles between their spring-calving grounds and their winter-feeding grounds.[1] These seasonal travels are called *migrations*. Woodland caribou live in much smaller herds of five to forty animals. They now live only in the forested bogs and mountains of northern Idaho and north-eastern Washington, and in Canada. Woodland caribou travel much shorter distances than barren ground caribou. They move only twenty to sixty miles as the seasons change. Caribou are bigger than most deer but smaller than elk and moose, the largest members of the deer family. A typical male (bull) woodland caribou weighs between 400 and 500 pounds. A female (cow) is smaller, weighing 300 pounds on average.[2]

▶ A Coat for All Seasons

Caribou are mammals. A mammal is a warm-blooded animal, which means it is able to control its own body temperature. When a mammal is too cold, it can warm itself by moving around and shivering. When a mammal gets too hot, it releases body heat by sweating and by breathing deeply and rapidly. Like all mammals, caribou give birth to live babies (calves) who drink their mother's milk and have some form of fur. Caribou are covered with a thick coat of fur that protects them from the wind and the cold.

Woodland caribou usually have brown and white coats. The fur on their faces and backs is dark brown, while the fur on their necks, undersides, and rumps is white. Caribou calves have the same markings as adults. Their coats are made up of two kinds of hair. Closest to their skin is a soft, wooly layer of underfur. Over the underfur is a thick layer of guard hairs. Each guard hair is hollow and filled with air. The dense underfur insulates the caribou,

holding in the animal's body heat. The hollow guard hairs protect the caribou from the elements, keeping rain, snow, and wind from reaching the caribou's skin. The extra air in their coats also helps caribou float when they are swimming. In the warm summer, the caribou sheds its wooly undercoat. This is called *molting*.

▶ Amazing Headgear

All male deer grow antlers except for one primitive species, the Chinese water deer. Antlers are what separate the deer family from other mammals. Antlers grow from the top of a deer's head. They are made of bone. Antlers are

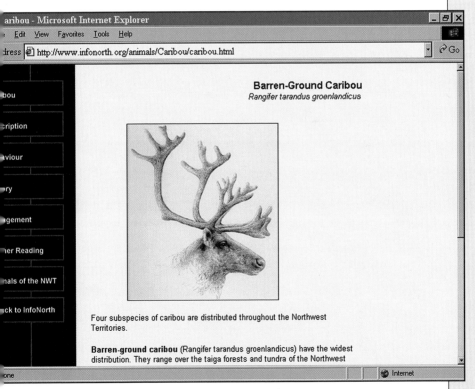

▲ The woodland caribou's antlers are used for protecting their young and fighting other caribou during rutting season.

branched, and, in woodland caribou, they can grow to 60 inches long.[3] Caribou are unique among North American deer, because the females also grow antlers. Every year the caribou grows a new set of antlers. Bulls shed their antlers in the winter and cows shed theirs in the spring. During the summer, new stubs sprout on the caribou's head. These stubby new antlers are covered with furry skin called *velvet*. The velvet carries blood and nutrients to the growing antlers. When the antlers are fully developed in the autumn, the velvet is no longer needed. It separates from the antler as the caribou scratches its antlers against small trees and shrubs. When the velvet wears off the shiny bone of a new antler rack appears.

Caribou use their antlers to protect themselves from predators. With their heads lowered, they charge at their enemies. The sight of an angry cow protecting its calf is enough to make most predators think twice about going after the easy meal of a weak calf.

Male caribou use their antlers primarily for fighting other bulls. Once their antlers are fully developed in the autumn, males are ready for the *rutting* season. The season lasts from early to mid-October. During this time, the males compete to determine who is strongest. They show off their antlers as a sign of their strength and battle with each other if there is any doubt which animal is more powerful. The strongest bulls mate with the cows to produce the next year's calves. This ensures that the best genes are passed on to future generations of caribou.

After the rutting season is over, male caribou shed their antlers. Pregnant cows keep their antlers until the spring, when the calves are born. Keeping their antlers longer allows pregnant cows to compete for the best food. Pregnant animals need extra food to nourish their growing

babies. Studies also show that female hormones remain at higher levels when antlers are present.

In Search of Food

Woodland caribou have a diverse diet. Lichens are their main food source. Lichens are plant-like growths of fungus and algae found on rocks and trees. Because lichens are tough to digest and have little nutritional value, few other animals eat lichens. Caribou also browse on the grasses, sedges, and mosses that grow in bogs (wet, spongy acres of ground) and on the forest floor. They nibble the bark and leaves of shrubs and young willow and birch trees. In the

tp://www.wa.gov/wdfw/wlm/research/pics/caribou/carib16.jpg - Microsoft Internet Explorer

Edit   View   Favorites   Tools   Help

ress   http://www.wa.gov/wdfw/wlm/research/pics/caribou/carib16.jpg   Go

one   Internet

▲ *Caribou typically consume grasses, lichens, and mosses. This Caribou is wearing a radio collar so that scientists can monitor its habits.*

winter, their food sources disappear under the snow cover. While the snow is soft, caribou are able to dig down with their hooves to find food. When the snow crust becomes too hard to dig through, caribou must look elsewhere for their meals. Caribou also use snow as a ladder. In very deep snow, they can browse higher in trees and eat the lichens growing there. The unique design of their hooves allows them to walk on top of the snow, as if wearing snowshoes.

As with all deer, caribou have special stomachs with four chambers. When they eat, the food goes to a holding chamber. Later caribou regurgitate the food from the holding chamber back into their mouths. Then they spend time chewing the food to break it down. This process is known as "chewing their cud." Once they have chewed it well, they swallow again, sending the food down to another chamber

Two caribou look for food as they move along the banks of the Kongakut River in Alaska.

where it is broken down even more by helpful bacteria. This allows caribou to eat as much as they want as quickly as possible, out in the open where there may be predators. They can then find a safer spot to chew and digest later. Animals that chew their cud are called *ruminants*. All deer, sheep, and domestic cows are ruminants.

Creative Communication

Caribou are quiet animals. Adults generally do not use their voices to communicate with each other. Calves and their mothers do, though. The cows call to their babies with a low grunting sound. The calves answer with a higher-pitched bleating cry. Although they rarely use their voices, caribou still use sound to communicate. As caribou walk, tendons moving over a bone in their feet make a clicking noise that can be heard from a distance of up to thirty feet. This noise helps to keep the caribou herd together. It may help calves find their family. Caribou also use scent glands to communicate with each other. The glands are located on their legs, faces, on the bottoms of their feet, and beneath their tails. When frightened, the caribou lifts its tail in warning and releases an alarm scent to alert other caribou of danger. During rutting season, caribou cows release a scent in their urine, which lets bulls know they are ready to mate.

Four Useful Tools

To better understand the animal world, biologists have grouped animals that are alike into categories. Caribou belong to the order *Artiodactyla*. This order, or category, includes goats, antelopes, and pigs, as well as the deer family, where caribou belong. All members of this order have even-toed hooves.

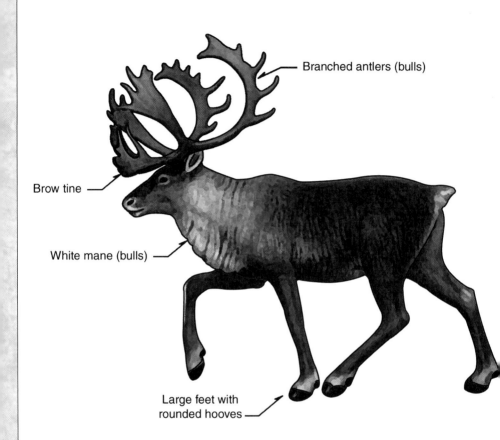

Branched antlers (bulls)

Brow tine

White mane (bulls)

Large feet with
rounded hooves

Caribou are part of the order of even-toed hoofed mammals, called *Artiodactyla*. Others in this order include antelope, goats, pigs, and the rest of the deer family. Caribou have four toes on each foot—two large and two small. Their large, broad cleft hooves are really the two large toes covered by a hard, bony substance. These wide hooves act like snowshoes, spreading the animal's weight over a large area. Behind the hooves are the two smaller toes, or *dewclaws*, which provide additional support. These special hooves allow caribou to walk on ice and snow in the winter and through soft bogs in the summer. In the winter, caribou also use their hooves like shovels to dig down under the snow to find food. Caribou calves can walk within an hour of birth, and they can outrun a human when they are only one day old.

Sometimes hungry caribou swim across rivers and lakes to get to better food supplies. Their hooves act as paddles, helping them to move through the current and stay afloat. The calves are even able to swim soon after birth.

Chapter 3 ▶

Shrinking Numbers

Wild animals live in a tough world with many dangers. Insects, hunters, disease, and shrinking habitats are but a few. Young caribou are especially at risk. They do not hide like other deer but instead follow their mothers. The defenseless calves can be an easy meal for a hungry wolf or bear.

▶ Nature's Threats

When the weather warms up in the spring, caribou shed their heavy winter coats. They lose tufts of fur and their hides look spotty and ragged. Mosquitoes are hatching at this time of year. They take advantage of the caribou's less-protected hide. Sometimes there are so many insects that an unlucky caribou can lose up to half a pint of blood in one day! This dangerously weakens the animal, which may already be weak from the long winter. If caribou are near a water source, they escape from the biting insects by swimming. Windy places offer relief as well. Here the mosquitoes are blown away. Caribou will also rest on large patches of snow to get away from insects.

Brainworm is another threat. Brainworm is a parasite carried by white-tailed deer. A parasite spends part of its lifetime either in or on another creature called a host. Parasites are not always harmful to their host. Brainworm does not seem to hurt white-tailed deer, but it is fatal in caribou. The worm causes brain damage in caribou and

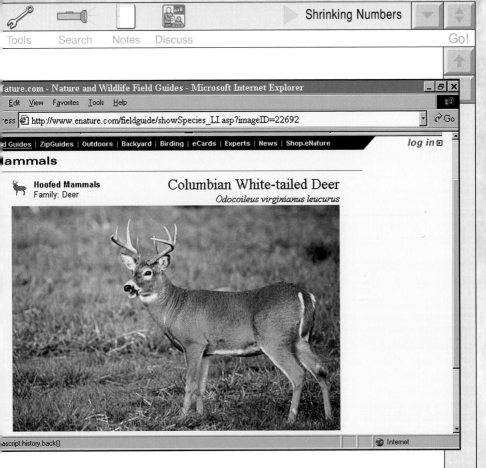

Nature.com - Nature and Wildlife Field Guides - Microsoft Internet Explorer

Edit View Favorites Tools Help

http://www.enature.com/fieldguide/showSpecies_LI.asp?imageID=22692 Go

d Guides | ZipGuides | Outdoors | Backyard | Birding | eCards | Experts | News | Shop.eNature   log in ▷

Mammals

Hoofed Mammals
Family: Deer

Columbian White-tailed Deer
Odocoileus virginianus leucurus

javascript:history.back()   Internet

⚠ *The Columbian white-tailed deer was listed as endangered in 1967. Since a refuge was established for the deer in 1972, however, it has made a major recovery.*

eventually death. When white-tailed deer and caribou populations meet, caribou are at risk for brainworm.

▷ Hunters' Market

Hunting was one reason for the decline of woodland caribou. The caribou were easy targets, because they lived in the same areas throughout the year. They do not always run away from people. Some people have reported caribou walking right up to them, close enough to swat on the nose![1]

Caribou meat was an important source of food for American Indians of the region. They made good use of

the caribou carcasses.[2] They used the furs for blankets, clothing, and shelter. They carved the antlers into tools such as knives and fishing hooks. Early settlers from Europe also hunted the caribou for food. They depended on the meat for survival.

▲ *Hunting woodland caribou is outlawed, but some still hunt other caribou for food or sport.*

As America grew, some people began hunting in a new way. These market hunters shot more animals than they themselves could use. They sent the meat to markets to be sold as food to other Americans. Market hunters killed as many animals as they possibly could. More meat meant more money in their pockets. Sometimes the meat rotted before it could be sold. This type of hunting was wasteful. Many caribou were slaughtered. Like the plains bison, woodland caribou were targets for the market hunters.

Hunting may have been a reason for the decline of caribou in the past. However, it is no longer a major threat. Hunting of woodland caribou is now outlawed in most places. Occasionally, a hunter mistakes a caribou for an elk, moose, or another deer. Poaching, or illegal hunting, of caribou is not common. It accounts for only a few deaths each year.

▶ Unwanted Guests

A caribou is a good meal for a wolf, bear, or cougar. It is natural for these meat-eating predators to attack caribou. Caribou are not helpless against predators. A healthy adult can outrun a wolf or bear. Predators can play an important role in keeping a caribou herd healthy. They attack sick and diseased animals because they are weak and easy to catch. More food is then available for the healthier caribou. Predators can also be very dangerous when a herd is small or weak. A herd of endangered animals may not be able to afford the loss of even one animal.

Lumber operations bring more predators to the caribou's territory. When there are openings in the forest, young trees have more space to grow. Moose and deer like to eat the new growth of leaves and buds from the small trees. Wolves and mountain lions follow after their

http://interactive.usask.ca/SKinteractive/modules/media/stills/tourism/prov_parks/moose_mtn/moo - Micr...

File   Edit   View   Favorites   Tools   Help

Address /interactive.usask.ca/SKinteractive/modules/media/stills/tourism/prov_parks/moose_mtn/moose_mtn01.jpg

Done   Internet

▲ *Lumber operations threaten the safety of the woodland caribou, because it brings predators into the forests where they live. The building of roads also causes problems for the caribou, because the roads cut into the caribou's habitat.*

food source—the deer and moose. These animals will also travel on the roads left by the lumber operations.[3]

Roads are a problem for many species. They cut into the animals' habitat. Cars sometimes hit animals as they cross roads. In northern climates, salt is spread along roads to keep them free of ice. Caribou and other animals like to lick the salt and will stand in the path of traffic.

Woodland caribou face many changes. They now share their northern forests with humans, roads, other deer, moose, and predators. Caribou do not adapt well to these changes. The lichens they eat only grow on older trees, not on the young trees that thrive after logging. It can take 80–150 years before a young forest grows the lichens that caribou eat.[4]

Shrinking Habitat

In the last hundred years, woodland caribou have retreated north, away from human development. Some scientists think the changing temperature of the planet is partly to blame. The earth's atmosphere is heating up. Many people think the gases from factories, airplanes, and cars are causing the warming. The warmer temperatures are changing the plants that make up America's forests. Caribou eat

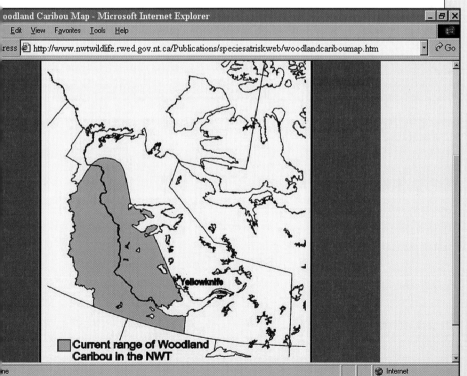

oodland Caribou Map - Microsoft Internet Explorer

Edit   View   Favorites   Tools   Help

ress   http://www.nwtwildlife.rwed.gov.nt.ca/Publications/speciesatriskweb/woodlandcariboumap.htm   Go

Yellowknife

Current range of Woodland Caribou in the NWT

▲ This map shows the current range of the woodland caribou in Canada's North West Territory.

specific plants and lichens, which only grow in certain areas. They may no longer be able to live in parts of their old habitat, because the food they need no longer grows there.

Farming also brings big changes to the land. Forests are cleared to make fields for agricultural crops. Farmers turn forests into grassy pastures where cows and sheep may graze. They build fences to keep their livestock from roaming free. The fences may also keep wild animals out. Fences can be a problem when there is not enough land for both the domestic and wild animals to share. Woodland caribou have not done well in areas where people have tamed the land. Caribou need forests where their main food source of lichens can grow undisturbed.[5]

Regardless of the reason, the shrinking number of caribou is a real cause for concern. Extinction caused by overdevelopment, disease, or natural predators is still extinction. Efforts to bring a halt to the shrinking numbers of woodland caribou in Washington, Idaho, and Canada are crucial.

People Decide to Help

North America has changed during the past two hundred years. People tamed the forests and prairies and used them for farmland. They hunted wildlife for food and for sport. Cities and towns grew. Roads and railroad tracks criss-crossed the country, often passing through the habitat of local wildlife. Some animals were able to adapt to such changes. Other animals, like the plains bison, suffered near extinction in the wild. Many animals would be lost forever to all Americans if the issues threatening wildlife were not addressed.

▶ The Endangered Species Act

Biologists and concerned citizens who understood what was happening worked hard to spread the word about the danger to America's native wildlife. They knew that animals and plants were, and still are, important to every American. However, these resources are limited and require protection if they are to be shared with future generations.

In 1973, Americans made a tough choice. The United States Congress passed the Endangered Species Act (ESA). This law has been updated several times. It is still in effect today. It protects any animals or plants that are *endangered* or *threatened*. Any animal or plant species that is in danger of extinction throughout all or a significant portion of its range is referred to as endangered. The phrase *threatened species* referred to any species that is likely to become an endangered species within the foreseeable future.[1] It is

▲ *The woodland caribou was placed on the U.S. Fish and Wildlife Service Endangered Species list in 1983.*

against the law to hunt endangered animals or to cut or take endangered plants.

The Endangered Species Act does more than outlaw such activities. It also says that we must help these species to recover. The United States government now keeps a list of all species, worldwide, that are in danger of extinction.

▶ Dwindling Populations

To recover, endangered animal populations need to stop shrinking. They must start to grow. In order to grow, the species must have more births than deaths. Animal babies, however, are weak. Even in the best conditions, not all baby animals survive. They are also easy targets for predators.

Captive breeding programs are one way people are helping. In a captive breeding program, animals give birth to their babies under the careful watch of humans. The babies are kept safe from danger while they grow strong. When they are old enough, the animals may be released into the wild. In the 1990s, biologists in the state of Washington raised a herd of eight woodland caribou calves in captivity. When the caribou were old enough, the biologists took them out into the forest. There they watched the feeding habits of the tame animals. Their goal was to understand what wild woodland caribou need to survive in Washington.[2]

▶ Radio Collars

Habitat loss is a major threat to woodland caribou. Caribou prefer to live far away from people, so little is known about their habitat needs. Even when biologists can find the shy animals, woodland caribou run away quickly. They are difficult to follow. A radio collar is a very useful tool for gathering information about animals in the wild. The collar sends out a signal that can be tracked by satellite. The trick is to get the collar around the animal's neck!

One team of biologists in Ontario, Canada, spent five days collaring a woodland caribou cow. They hoped to monitor the cow's movements during the spring calving season. The biologists walked slowly through the woods, herding the caribou before them. To avoid the team, the wary caribou tried to swim to an island in a nearby lake. Other team members carefully approached the swimming caribou by boat. They successfully put a radio collar on the surprised animal.[3] Another technique for collaring wild

caribou is shooting a net over the animal from a helicopter. Once the animal is caught in the net, biologists may safely approach the caribou to attach the collar.[4]

Wildlife Refuges

Endangered animals need a safe place to live. Their habitat is often threatened. Wildlife refuges are one way that people help endangered species. The word *refuge* means a place that is safe from danger. A wildlife refuge is a protected place for animals to live. The United States has over 93 million acres set aside as wildlife refuges. One of these is the Arctic National Wildlife Refuge in Alaska. A huge herd of more than 129,000 barren ground caribou lives there. Unlike

These caribou are frolicking in the Arctic National Wildlife Refuge in Alaska. They are most likely looking for cotton grass to eat.

their woodland caribou cousins, barren ground caribou are not endangered. Humans have not disturbed their habitat. This may soon change. The Arctic National Wildlife Refuge has recently been the source of many debates in Washington, D.C. In 2001, legislators introduced a bill in Congress that would allow oil drilling in this wildlife refuge.

Caribou with velvet on its antlers. ▷

Conservationists are extremely concerned. The presence of humans, roads, and machinery would disturb the herd of barren ground caribou. The oil drilling would take place on the same coastal plains where caribou give birth to their calves each spring.[5]

Help From a Neighbor

There are many more woodland caribou in Canada than there are in the United States. Yet the caribou's habitat is at risk in Canada, too. The most endangered herds live on two mountains in the Gaspé region of the province of Quebec. The mountains are in a national park called the Parc de la Gaspésie. The Canadian Wildlife Service listed the Gaspésie herds of woodland caribou as threatened in 1984. Their status was upgraded to endangered in 2002.

Woodland caribou began to decline in Quebec during the mid-1900s. People changed the caribou habitat with logging and agriculture. Hunting also affected the caribou's numbers. By the 1970s, fewer than two hundred caribou survived in the Gaspé region of Quebec. Bears and coyotes became a major problem for the weakened herds. They preyed on the calves. In some years, the predators killed nine out of ten calves. With those odds, the caribou would never survive. To protect the caribou herds, biologists began trapping coyotes in the 1990s. With fewer predators the caribou herds slowly began to grow.[6]

Chapter 5

The Future of the Woodland Caribou

By the 1980s, woodland caribou were in serious trouble in the United States. Only twenty-five caribou were left in the Selkirk Mountains in the northwest. Woodland caribou long had been extinct in the northeastern United States. Even so, biologists in Maine decided to attempt a recovery plan. They wanted to reintroduce the species to

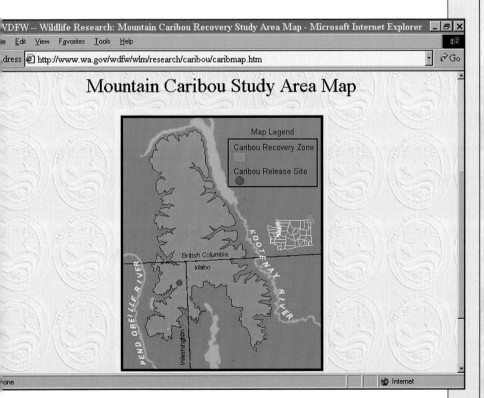

WDFW -- Wildlife Research: Mountain Caribou Recovery Study Area Map - Microsoft Internet Explorer

e Edit View Favorites Tools Help

dress http://www.wa.gov/wdfw/wlm/research/caribou/caribmap.htm   Go

Mountain Caribou Study Area Map

Map Legend

Caribou Recovery Zone

Caribou Release Site

British Columbia

Idaho

Washington

PEND OREILLE RIVER

KOOTENAY RIVER

▲ This map shows the recovery zones and release sites of caribou in the northwestern United States and British Columbia, Canada.

their state. They would take animals from a healthy herd in Canada. Then they would release the animals in the Maine woods, where they used to live eighty years ago.[1]

Maine Caribou Experiment

At one time the northern forests of Maine had been undisturbed by humans. The boggy woods were home to woodland caribou and moose. In the 1800s, lumberjacks changed the face of the land when they cut down trees for timber. These woods had never seen such change before. It was too much for some of the animals. By the early 1900s, the caribou were gone, and the moose were struggling to survive.

▲ *A moose calf leaving the water in Baxter State Park. Scientists tried to breed woodland caribou there in 1990.*

Moose began to rebound in Maine during the 1970s. People thought that if moose could come back, maybe caribou could, too. So, in 1986, scientists captured thirty-five woodland caribou from a herd in Newfoundland, Canada. The caribou were taken to the University of Maine at Orono. Only twenty survived the journey. They were kept in pens while the herd grew. The plan was to release the caribou into the Maine woods. Scientists fitted the caribou with radio collars, which would allow people to track the animals in the wild.

In 1989 and 1990, the caribou were released into the wild. Baxter State Park, in Maine, would be their new home. Everyone anxiously waited to see how the animals would do. The scientists followed the caribou by tracking their radio collar signals. They were not happy with what they learned. One by one the caribou died. Many died of brainworm, the parasite carried by white-tailed deer; others became prey for black bears and coyotes. Sadly, the effort to restore caribou to Maine failed.

▷ Selkirk Mountains Herd in Jeopardy

In 1984, fewer than thirty woodland caribou were left in the Selkirk Mountains. That year, the U.S. Fish and Wildlife Service put woodland caribou on the Endangered Species List. Woodland caribou could not be reintroduced in Maine, but biologists are working to save the Selkirk herd from extinction. Together, the University of Idaho, U.S. Fish and Wildlife Service, and Canadian Fish and Wildlife have taken caribou from British Columbia and added them to the Selkirk Mountains herd. Since 1987, biologists have transplanted more than one hundred caribou from British Columbia to Idaho and Washington.[2] Yet in March 2000, the herd numbered only thirty-two.

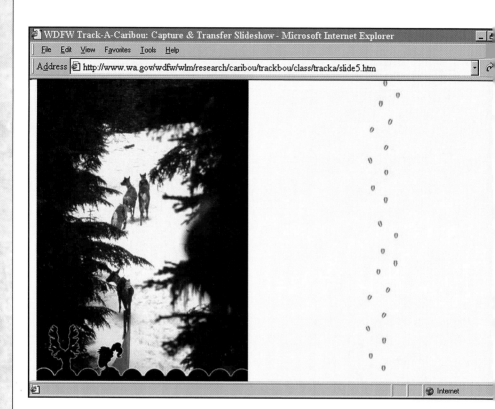

WDFW Track-A-Caribou: Capture & Transfer Slideshow - Microsoft Internet Explorer

File   Edit   View   Favorites   Tools   Help

Address http://www.wa.gov/wdfw/wlm/research/caribou/trackbou/class/tracka/slide5.htm

Since the 1960s, the woodland caribou population in the United States has been restricted to the Selkirk Mountains of the northwestern United States and British Columbia, Canada. Pictured here is a herd of caribou in the Selkirk Mountains.

That is sixteen fewer than the previous census. According to Mark Sprengel of Selkirk-Priest Basin Association, an environmental activist group, the herd's survival is in serious jeopardy.[3]

Today, though the Selkirk herd still exists, it remains in danger. In the summer of 2001, a proposed 15-mile-long road project became the focus of concern in the Selkirk ecosystem. Biologists disagree about how to help the caribou. Some people think the Selkirk Mountains must be left alone if the caribou are to survive. Others feel that the forests must be carefully managed and the caribou will do well. Only time will tell which, if either, of these approaches will work. By then it may be too late. Unless woodland caribou are given immediate attention, they are in danger of extinction. Other animals in the Selkirk ecosystem that are threatened include "bull trout, gray wolves, lynx," and about forty grizzly bears.[4]

Unknown Future

Many people do not even know that woodland caribou exist. Those who do know may not realize that they are in trouble. The Selkirk caribou are evidence of how difficult it can be to help animals threatened by extinction. Learning the cause for an animal population's decline does

▲ *The grizzly bear is another species threatened by activity in the Selkirk Mountains.*

not insure its protection. It is also important to share what you have learned, to "get the word out."

Most endangered species are at risk, because people have altered the species' habitat. Learning from past mistakes is the key to helping wildlife in the future. It is much easier to save an animal before it reaches the brink of extinction. It is even better to conserve habitats so that animals and plants do not need to be saved. To *conserve* means to protect and use wisely. Recycling is one way to conserve. When people use recycled paper, for example, that helps to conserve forests.

When people decide to act responsibly, they can change things for the better. Choosing leaders who are

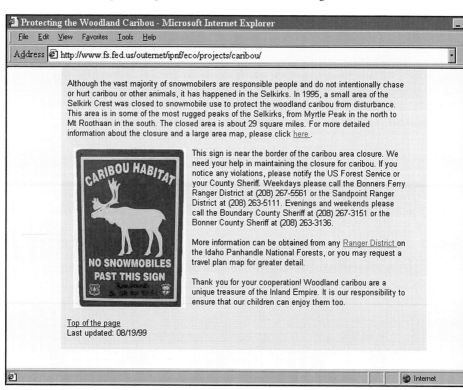

Protecting the Woodland Caribou - Microsoft Internet Explorer

File   Edit   View   Favorites   Tools   Help

Address http://www.fs.fed.us/outernet/ipnf/eco/projects/caribou/

Although the vast majority of snowmobilers are responsible people and do not intentionally chase or hurt caribou or other animals, it has happened in the Selkirks. In 1995, a small area of the Selkirk Crest was closed to snowmobile use to protect the woodland caribou from disturbance. This area is in some of the most rugged peaks of the Selkirks, from Myrtle Peak in the north to Mt Roothaan in the south. The closed area is about 29 square miles. For more detailed information about the closure and a large area map, please click here .

CARIBOU HABITAT

NO SNOWMOBILES
PAST THIS SIGN

This sign is near the border of the caribou area closure. We need your help in maintaining the closure for caribou. If you notice any violations, please notify the US Forest Service or your County Sheriff. Weekdays please call the Bonners Ferry Ranger District at (208) 267-5561 or the Sandpoint Ranger District at (208) 263-5111. Evenings and weekends please call the Boundary County Sheriff at (208) 267-3151 or the Bonner County Sheriff at (208) 263-3136.

More information can be obtained from any Ranger District on the Idaho Panhandle National Forests, or you may request a travel plan map for greater detail.

Thank you for your cooperation! Woodland caribou are a unique treasure of the Inland Empire. It is our responsibility to ensure that our children can enjoy them too.

Top of the page
Last updated: 08/19/99

Internet

Signs like this one help protect the woodland caribou's habitat.

concerned about America's natural resources is something every voter can do. Political leaders play an important role in conservation. They make decisions that can change the lives of endangered species. After all, it was Congress that passed the Endangered Species Act. Most students may not be old enough to vote, but they can talk with their family and friends. They can tell them what they have learned. Change happens when people work together.

People who care about threatened animals worldwide are already working together to conserve animal habitats. They belong to international and national conservation groups. These groups teach people about endangered animals, raise money to buy land for wildlife habitat, and write letters to political leaders urging them to vote favorably on issues concerning the future of native wildlife. Regional or local groups may provide opportunities for you to learn about or even to work with endangered animals near where you live.

The Endangered and Threatened Wildlife List

This series is based on the Endangered and Threatened Wildlife list compiled by the U.S. Fish and Wildlife Service (USFWS). Each book explores an endangered or threatened animal, tells why it has become endangered or threatened, and explains the efforts being made to restore the species' population.

The United States Fish and Wildlife Service, in the Department of the Interior, and the National Marine Fisheries Service, in the Department of Commerce, share responsibility for administration of the Endangered Species Act.

In 1973, Congress took the farsighted step of creating the Endangered Species Act, widely regarded as the world's strongest and most effective wildlife conservation law. It set an ambitious goal: to reverse the alarming trend of human-caused extinction that threatened the ecosystems we all share.

The complete list of Endangered and Threatened Wildlife and Plants can be found at **http://endangered.fws.gov/wildlife.html#Species**

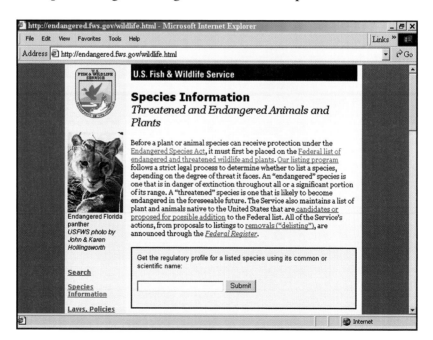

Chapter Notes

Chapter 1. The Vanishing Caribou

1. David Lee, "Caribou and You," *American Forests*, vol. 101, no. 7–8, July-August 1995, p. 45.

Chapter 2. What Is the Woodland Caribou?

1. U.S. Fish and Wildlife Service, "Arctic National Wildlife Refuge," November 16, 2000, <http://www.r7.fws .gov/nwr/arctic/caribou.html> (June 15, 2002).

2. Washington Department of Fish and Wildlife, "Track-A-Caribou Overview: Caribou Introduction," 1998, <http://www.wa.gov/wdfw/wlm/research/caribou/trackbou/ class/overview/family.htm> (June 30, 2002).

3. William Henry Burt, *Mammals, Peterson's Field Guides of North America Series* (Boston: Houghton Mifflin, 1980), p. 220.

Chapter 3. Shrinking Numbers

1. John Madson, "Bringing the 'bou Back to its Old Stomping Grounds," *Smithsonian,* vol. 22, no. 2, May 1991, p. 102.

2. U.S. Fish and Wildlife Service, "Caribou: Rangifer tarandus caribou," August 1998, <http://www/nctc.fws.gov/ library/Pubs/caribou.pdf> (June 30, 2002).

3. Doug Charrett, "Secretive and Rare: The Woodland Caribou," *Saskatchewan Naturally Magazine*, April 1999, <http://www.becquet.com/naturally/caribou.htm> (June 30, 2002).

4. "Woodland Caribou: Food," June 17, 2002, <http:// www3.gov.ab.ca/srd/fw/threatsp/wcar_food.html> (July 25, 2002).

5. Canadian Wildlife Service, "Hinterland Who's Who: Caribou," 1992, <http://www.cws-scf.ec.gc.ca/hww-fap/ hww-fap.cfm?ID_species=55&lang=e> (June 15, 2002).

Chapter 4. People Decide to Help

1. U.S. Fish and Wildlife Service, "ESA Basics," n.d., <http://endangered.fws.gov/esa.html> (June 23, 2001).

2. David Lee, "Caribou and You," *American Forests*, vol. 101, no. 7–8, July-August 1995, p. 45.

3. Ontario Parks Magazine, "Science: Collaring Caribou is Wet Work," n.d., <http://www.ontarioparks.com/parkzine/parkzine.html#> (June 15, 2002).

4. Washington Department of Fish and Wildlife, "Wildlife Research: Caribou Recovery Process," n.d., <http://www.wa.gov/wdfw/wlm/research/caribou/caribou.htm#caribounetting> (June 30, 2002).

5. Tom McGuire, "Emergency Wildlife Appeal–Arctic National Wildlife Refuge," n.d., <http://www.nwf.org/enews/arctic01.html> (June 23, 2002).

6. Environment Canada, "Species at Risk: Woodland Caribou," April 27, 2001, <http://www.speciesatrisk.gc.ca/species/English/SearchDetail.cfm?SpeciesID=144#note> (June 23, 2002).

Chapter 5. The Future of Woodland Caribou

1. John Madson, "Bringing the 'bou Back to its Old Stomping Ground," *Smithsonian*, vol. 22, no. 2, May 1991, p. 103.

2. Washington Department of Fish and Wildlife, "Track–A-Caribou: Caribou Overview, Transplants," n.d., <http://www.wa.gov/wdfw/wlm/research/caribou/trackbou/class/overview/transp.htm> (June 18, 2002).

3. "The Caribou's Last Stand?" featured in In Brief, *E Magazine (The Environmental Magazine)*, vol. 11, no. 4, July-August 2000, p. 14.

4. Jacob Goldstein, "At the Brink: The Selkirk Grizzlies," *Wildlife Conservation*, vol. 105, no. 3, June 2002, p. 22.

Further Reading

Ahlstrom, Mark E. *The Pronghorn.* Mankato, Minn.: Crestwood House, 1986.

Doyle, Dan. *Buffalo.* Danbury, Conn.: Grolier Educational, 1997.

Harris, Lorle K. *The Caribou.* Minneapolis, Minn.: Dillon Press, Inc., 1988.

Hodge, Deborah. *Deer, Moose, Elk and Caribou.* Toronto, Ont.: Kids Can Press, 1998.

Marshall Cavendish Corporation. *Endangered Wildlife of the World,* vol. 1–11. New York: Marshall Cavendish, 1993.

Masuzumi, Alfred. *Caribou Hide: Two Stories of Life on the Land.* Yellowknife, N.W.T., Canada: Raven Rock Publishing, 1999.

Nentl, Jerolyn Ann. *The Caribou.* Mankato, Minn.: Crestwood House, 1984.

Turbak, Gary. *Mountain Animals in Danger.* Flagstaff, Ariz.: Northland Publishing, 1994.

Walker, Tom. *Caribou: Wanderer of the Tundra.* Portland, Oreg.: Graphic Arts Center Publishing Company, 2000.

Wassink, Jan L. *Idaho Wildlife.* Helena, Mont.: Farcountry Press, 1987.

Woodward, John. *Bison.* Danbury, Conn.: Grolier Educational, 2001.

Zwaschka, Michael. *The White-Tailed Deer.* Mankato, Minn.: Capstone Press, 1997.